AN EDUCATIONAL COUNTRY TRAVEL PICTURE BOOK FOR KIDS ABOUT HISTORY, DESTINATION PLACES, ANIMALS AND MANY MORE

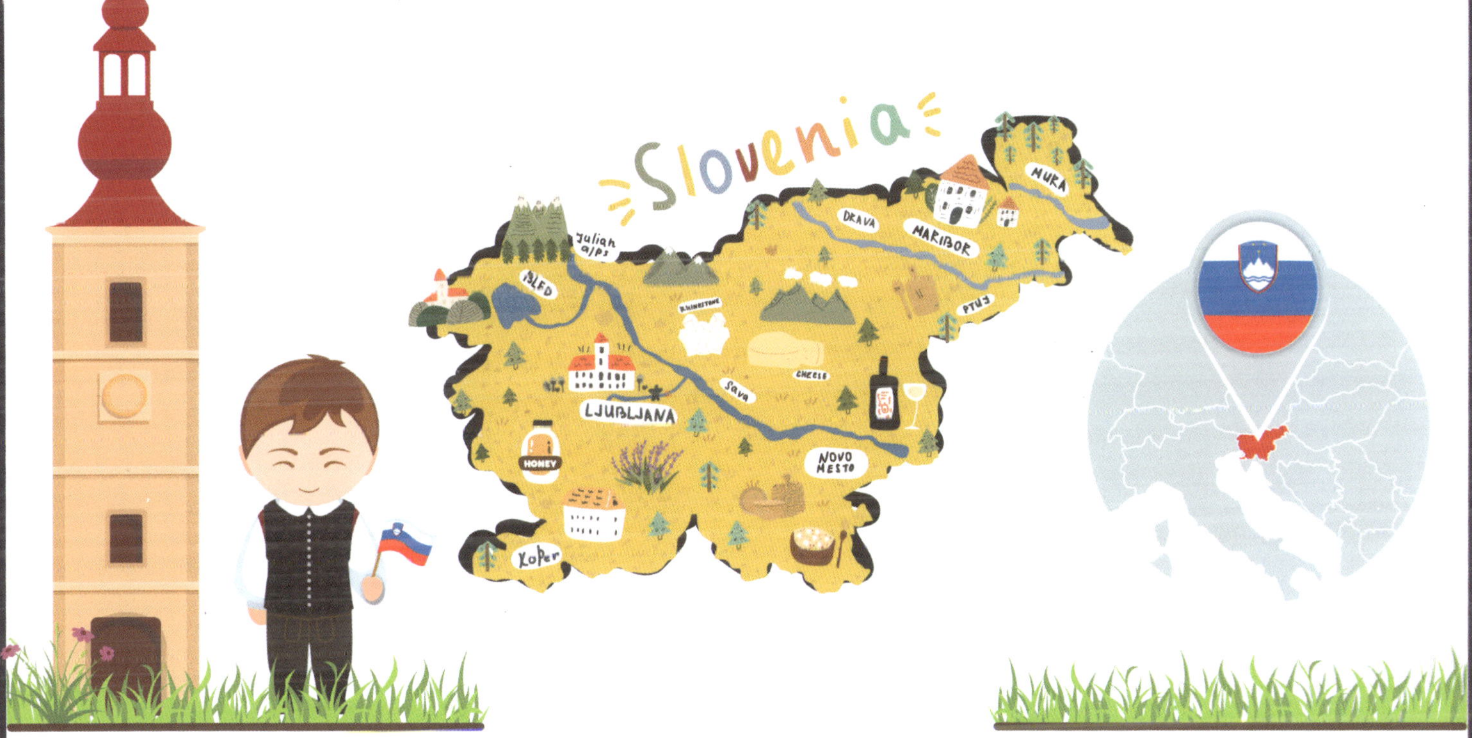

Slovenia is a small country located in Central Europe.

Which continent does Slovenia belong to?

Slovenia is in Europe.

How many countries does Slovenia border?

Slovenia shares borders with four countries: Italy, Austria, Hungary, and Croatia.

How big is Slovenia?

Slovenia covers an area of approximately 20,273 square kilometers.

What percentage of the world's land does Slovenia occupy?

Slovenia occupies less than 0.05% of the world's land area.

Which city is the largest in Slovenia?

Ljubljana is the largest city and the capital of Slovenia.

Why do tourists visit Slovenia?

Tourists visit Slovenia for its beautiful natural landscapes, historic cities, outdoor activities, and cultural attractions. Popular destinations include Lake Bled, Ljubljana, and the Julian Alps.

What are the people of Slovenia called?

The people of Slovenia are called Slovenians.

What is the national animal of Slovenia?

The national animal of Slovenia is the Lipizzaner horse.

What is the national sport of Slovenia?

Alpine skiing is a popular and successful sport in Slovenia, but there is no official national sport.

What is the national tree of Slovenia?

The linden tree (Tilia) is often considered a symbol of Slovenia.

What is the official name of Slovenia?

The official name of Slovenia is the "Republic of Slovenia."

What is Slovenia's nickname?

Slovenia is often referred to as the "Green Heart of Europe" due to its lush natural landscapes.

It's known for its stunning natural landscapes, including the Julian Alps and the Karst Plateau.

Slovenia has a population of approximately 2 million people.

Ljubljana is the capital and largest city of Slovenia.

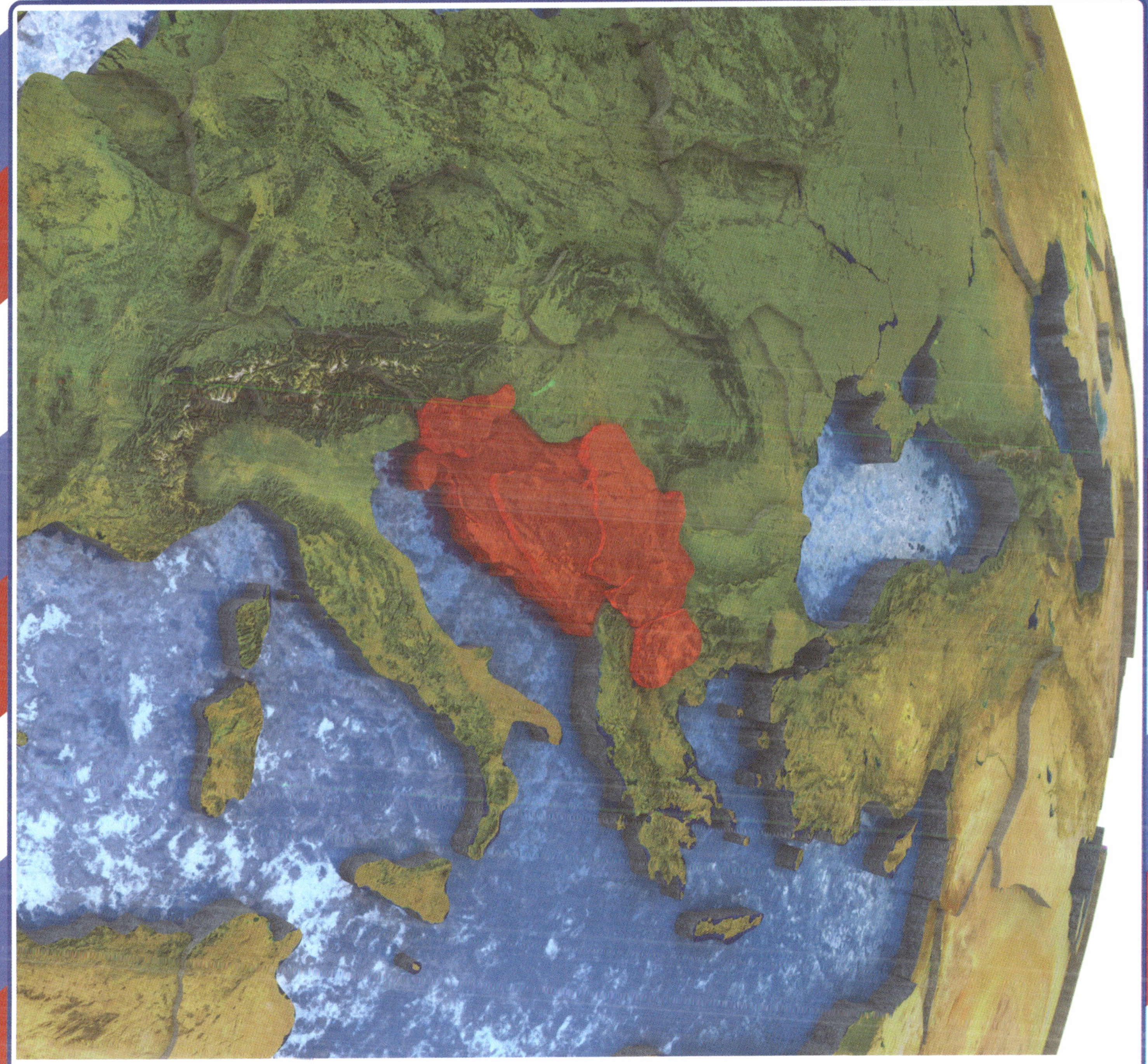

Slovenia was part of the former Yugoslavia before gaining independence in 1991.

The country is known for its excellent skiing and winter sports, with popular ski resorts in the Julian Alps.

Lake Bled is one of Slovenia's most famous tourist attractions, featuring a picturesque island with a church.

Slovenia is one of the world's most water-rich countries, with many rivers, including the Sava and Drava.

The country is famous for its extensive cave systems, with Postojna Cave being one of the most visited.

Slovenia is home to more than 13,000 caves.

The "Solkan Bridge" in Nova Gorica is the world's longest stone bridge-arch.

The traditional Slovenian dish is called "potica," a sweet roll filled with nuts or other fillings.

The brown bear is one of Slovenia's indigenous animals and can be seen in the country's forests.

Slovenia was the first country in the world to be declared a green destination by the Green Destinations organization.

The country has 46.6 kilometers of coastline along the Adriatic Sea.

Slovenia is known for its pristine nature and extensive forests, with nearly 60% of its land covered in forests.

The Triglav National Park is the only national park in Slovenia and is named after the country's highest peak, Mount Triglav.

Slovenia is famous for its beekeeping tradition and has beautifully painted beehives.

The Pletna boat is a traditional wooden boat used to transport visitors to Bled Island.

Bled Castle, perched on a cliff above Lake Bled, is one of the oldest castles in Slovenia.

Slovenians celebrate a carnival known as "Pust," with colorful masks and processions.

The world's oldest wooden wheel, dating back to around 3200 BC, was found in Ljubljana Marshes in Slovenia.

Slovenia is home to over 380 species of birds.

The country is a paradise for hikers and outdoor enthusiasts with many well-marked trails.

The Lipica Stud Farm is the oldest stud farm in the world and home to the Lipizzaner horses.

Slovenia has a rich cultural heritage, with many museums, galleries, and historic sites.

Slovenia is a great place for water sports, with many rivers and lakes for kayaking, rafting, and fishing.

The scenic Vintgar Gorge near Bled is a popular hiking destination.

The "Franja Marathon" is a famous international cycling race held in Slovenia.

The Ptuj Castle is one of the country's oldest castles, dating back to the 12th century.

Slovenia is known for its vibrant summer festivals, such as the Ana Desetnica International Street Theater Festival.

Slovenia is a popular destination for ecotourism, with a focus on sustainability and conservation.

The official language is Slovene.

The town of Piran is often compared to Venice for its charming streets and coastal location.

Slovenia is a member of the European Union and uses the Euro as its currency.

The highest ski resort in Slovenia is Kanin in the Julian Alps.

The country has a vibrant music scene, and one of the most famous music festivals is the Ljubljana Festival.

The famous artist Jože Plečnik has left a significant architectural legacy in Ljubljana.

The Predjama Castle is built into the mouth of a cave and is known for its dramatic location.

The Studor ethnological collection in Bohinj showcases traditional Slovenian life.

The country has a strong tradition of winter sports, including ski jumping and cross-country skiing.

Slovenia's flag features the national emblem, which includes Mount Triglav and a star.

Slovenia's flag consists of three horizontal stripes: white, blue, and red.

Slovenia is part of the Schengen Area, making it easy for travelers to visit neighboring countries.

The country is home to various thermal spas, making it a popular destination for relaxation and wellness.

The Karst region is famous for its unique limestone landscapes and underground caves.

The Idrija Lace is a traditional lace-making technique that is part of UNESCO's Intangible Cultural Heritage.

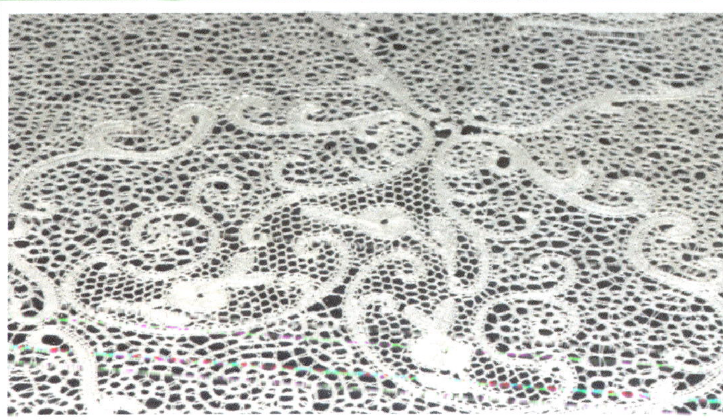

Slovenia is a great place for rock climbing and mountaineering, with numerous climbing routes.

TOP 10 TRAVEL TIPS FOR VISITING SLOVENIA

1. **Plan Ahead:** Before you go, research and plan your trip. Know the places you want to visit and how to get there.
2. **Weather:** Check the weather before you pack. Slovenia has different climates, so pack accordingly.
3. **Safety First:** Slovenia is generally safe, but still, take care of your belongings and stay in well-lit areas at night.
4. **Currency:** Slovenia uses the Euro (€). Make sure to have some cash and cards for payments.
5. **Language:** Learn a few basic Slovenian phrases, but most people in Slovenia speak English.
6. **Local Food:** Try traditional Slovenian dishes like potica and burek. Also, taste local wines.
7. **Nature:** Enjoy Slovenia's natural beauty. Go hiking, explore caves, and swim in crystal-clear lakes.
8. **Public Transport:** Use buses and trains for easy and affordable travel within the country.
9. **Respect Nature:** Keep Slovenia clean. Don't litter and stay on marked paths in national parks.
10. **Stay Connected:** Get a local SIM card or use Wi-Fi to stay connected and share your travel experiences.

Pros of visiting Slovenia:

1. **Beautiful Nature:** Slovenia is a very pretty country with mountains, lakes, and forests. If you like the outdoors, you'll love it here.
2. **Charming Cities:** The cities in Slovenia are nice to visit, with old buildings, cafes, and interesting things to see.
3. **Safe and Friendly:** It's a safe place to visit, and people are kind and helpful to tourists.

Cons of visiting Slovenia:

1. **Crowded Places:** Sometimes, the popular spots like Lake Bled can be very busy, and that might take away from the peaceful feeling.
2. **Transport Can Be Tricky:** While the cities have good buses and trains, getting around in some remote areas can be harder without a car.
3. **Unpredictable Weather:** The weather can change quickly, so you might need to deal with rain or unexpected weather changes, especially in the mountains.

Printed in Dunstable, United Kingdom